Help Me! Guide to the Ap

MW00946273

By Charles Hughes

Table of Contents

Getting Started

Table of Contents

1. What the Apple Watch Can and Cannot Do

While the Apple Watch is a versatile device that can perform many functions, there are certain limitations. However, you can use your iPhone to perform any functions that the Apple Watch cannot.

What the Apple Watch CAN Do

1. View email, text message, voice call, calendar, and application notifications.
2. Use Siri, Apple's voice assistant.
3. Set and track your fitness goals.
4. Use the watch as a wallet with Apple Pay.
5. Use Apple Watch-compatible applications.

What the Apple Watch CANNOT Do

1. Sync with Android or other smartphones. Currently, the Apple Watch can only sync with the iPhone 5, 5C, 5S, and 6.
2. Use a virtual keyboard to answer text messages.
3. Take pictures or capture videos.
4. Use GPS, Wi-Fi, or mobile data without a paired iPhone.
5. FaceTime calling.

2. Button Layout

The watch has four buttons. The rest of the functionality is controlled by the touchscreen.

Figure 1: Front View

- Digital Crown - Returns to the Home screen or the watch face. Launches Siri, zooms, scrolls, and adjusts settings.

- Side Button - Turns the watch on or off. Opens the Friends menu. Turns on Apple pay.

Band Release Button

Band Release Button

Figure 2: Rear View

- Band Release Buttons - Lets you slide out the watch band.

3. Setting Up

When you first take the Apple Watch out of the box, you need to pair it to your iPhone using Bluetooth. To pair your Apple Watch to your iPhone:

1. Press and hold the Side button. The Apple logo appears.
2. Select the language that you want to use on your watch. The Pairing screen appears, as shown in **Figure 3**.

3. Touch the ![watch icon] icon on your iPhone. The Apple Watch application opens, as shown in **Figure 4**. Ensure that Bluetooth is turned on on your iPhone. To turn on Bluetooth on your iPhone, touch the bottom of the screen and slide your finger up. Then, touch the ⓧ icon.

4. Touch **Start Pairing** on the watch and on the iPhone.

5. Line up the watch with the viewfinder. A confirmation screen appears, and the watch is paired with your iPhone.

6. Touch **Set Up as New Apple Watch** if you want to set up the watch from scratch, or touch **Restore from Backup** to set up the watch using the information on your existing iPhone.

7. Select your preferences on the following screens. Enter your Apple ID and password when prompted.

8. Touch **Install All** on the Install Available Apps screen to install any compatible applications on the watch. Otherwise, touch **Choose Later**. The watch syncs with your iPhone. When this process is complete, your watch is ready to use.

Figure 3: Pairing Screen

Figure 4: Apple Watch Application on the iPhone

4. Charging the Apple Watch

The watch comes with a wireless charger. Plug in the charger and lay the watch face up on the circular charging dock. The watch begins to charge, and a green lightning bolt appears at the top of the screen. A magnet holds the watch securely in place on the charging dock.

5. Turning the Apple Watch On or Off

To turn off the watch, press and hold the Side button. The Power screen appears, as shown

in **Figure 5**. Touch the ⏻ icon, and slide it to the right. The watch turns off. You can also use the Power Reserve feature to enable a low-power mode, which will conserve your battery. While in Power Reserve, you can only use the watch to tell the time. To exit Power Reserve mode, press and hold the Side button until the Apple logo appears.

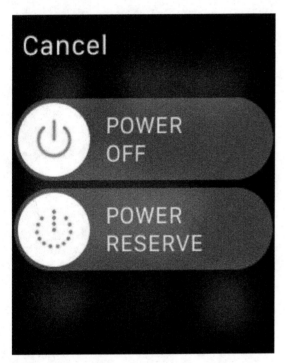

Figure 5: Power Screen

6. Waking Up the Apple Watch

There are several ways to wake up the watch. Press either of the buttons or touch the screen to wake up the screen. You can also turn your wrist to face you to turn on the screen, but only if the Wrist Raise feature is turned on. Refer to *"Adjusting Wrist Raise Settings"* on page 82 to learn how to turn on this feature.

7. Customizing the Clock

You can change the appearance of the clock. To change the face of the watch:
1. Press the screen firmly by applying slightly more pressure than when you tap it to select an item. The Face Customization screen appears, as shown in **Figure 6**.
2. Touch **Customize**. The Color screen appears, as shown in **Figure 7**.
3. Use the Digital Crown to adjust the color. Touch the screen and swipe to the left when you are finished. The Widget Customization screen appears, as shown in **Figure 8**.
4. Touch each widget on the screen, and use the Digital Crown to change it.
5. Press the Digital Crown. Your customization settings are saved.

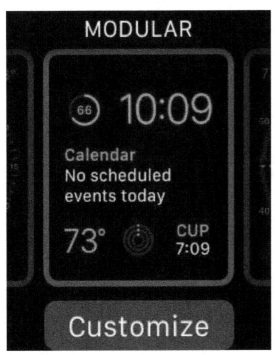

Figure 6: Face Customization Screen

Figure 7: Color Screen

Figure 8: Widget Customization Screen

Using Applications

Table of Contents

1. Opening an Application

To open an application on the watch, press the Digital Crown. The Home screen appears, as shown in **Figure 1**. Touch an application icon to open the corresponding application. You can also use the Digital Crown to zoom in or out on the Home screen. If you zoom in far enough on an application, the application opens. If you quickly zoom out before the application fully opens, you can return to the Home screen.

Figure 1: Home Screen

2. Rearranging Your Application Icons

You can customize your Home screen by rearranging application icons. To move an icon to another location, touch and hold it until all of the icons begin to shake. Drag the icon to its new location and release the screen. The icon is moved and the other icons are rearranged accordingly. Press the Digital Crown to accept the new icon position.

3. Installing an Application from the App Store

Use the Apple Watch application on your iPhone to install applications on the watch. To install an application from the App Store:

1. Touch the icon on your iPhone. The Apple Watch Application Home screen opens, as shown in **Figure 2**.
2. Touch **Featured** at the bottom of the screen. The Featured Applications screen appears, as shown in **Figure 3**. You can also touch **Search** at the bottom of the screen to search for a specific application.
3. Touch **GET** next to the name of an application, or touch the application icon to view the application description. 'INSTALL' appears. You can also touch **GET** on the Application Description screen. If the application is paid, touch the price of the application instead of touching 'GET'.
4. Touch **INSTALL**. The application is installed on your iPhone. You may need to enter your iTunes password before the download can begin. If you have Automatic Downloads turned on, the application is automatically installed on the watch. Otherwise, proceed to step 5.
5. Touch **My Watch** at the bottom of the screen. The My Watch Home screen appears.
6. Scroll down to the bottom of the list, and touch the newly installed application. The Application Settings screen appears.

7. Touch the switch next to **'Show App on Apple Watch'**. The application is installed on the watch. Some applications, such as Instagram, require that you log in to your account using your iPhone.

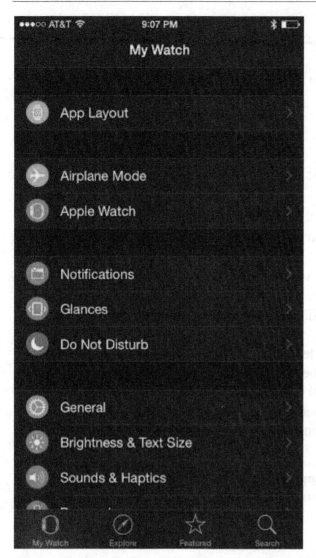

Figure 2: Apple Watch Application Home Screen on the iPhone

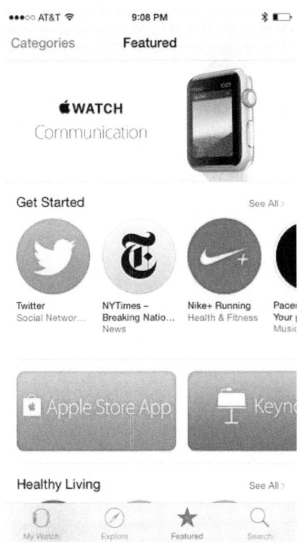

Figure 3: Featured Applications Screen on the iPhone

4. Deleting an Installed Application

You can customize your Home screen by deleting applications. When you delete an application, it is still installed on your iPhone, and you can restore it at any time. To delete an application icon:

- Touch and hold it until all of the icons begin to shake.
- Touch the X in the upper left-hand corner of the application icon. A confirmation screen appears.
- Touch **Delete App**. The application is deleted.

To restore the application:

1. Touch the icon on your iPhone. The Apple Watch Application Home screen opens.
2. Scroll down and touch the application that you want to restore. The Application Settings screen appears.

3. Touch the switch next to **'Show App on Apple Watch'**. The application is restored to the watch.

5. Returning to the Last Used Application

You can quickly return to the application that you last used by pressing the Digital Crown twice quickly.

Text Messaging

Table of Contents

1. Reading a New Text Message

You can read new text messages on your watch. By default, the text message notification appears on both your iPhone and your watch. When a new text message arrives, the New Text Message

Notification appears, as shown in **Figure 1**. Touch the ⬤ icon at the top of the screen. The Conversation screen appears, as shown in **Figure 2**.

Note: If you are using your iPhone, or the iPhone is awake, the new text message notification does not appear on the watch.

Figure 1: New Message Notification

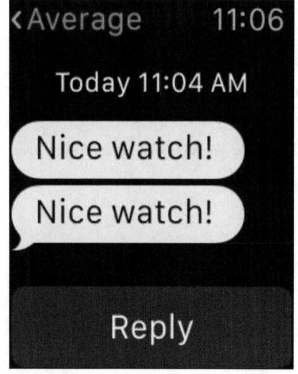

Figure 2: Conversation Screen

2. Viewing a Text Conversation

There are two methods to open a text conversation between you and a contact:

- Touch the ⬜ icon on the Home screen.

- Touch the ⬜ icon on the New Message Notification screen.

3. Viewing a Photo in a Text Message

If you receive a photo in a text message, you can view it on your watch. To view the photo in full-screen, as shown in **Figure 3**, touch it twice quickly. To return to the text conversation, touch the left side of the screen and move your finger to the right.

Figure 3: Photo in Full Screen

4. Viewing a Video in a Text Message

If you receive a video in a text message, as shown in **Figure 4**, you can watch it on your watch. Touch the video once to play it. Use the Digital Crown to control the volume. You can also view the video controls by touching the screen once while the video is playing.

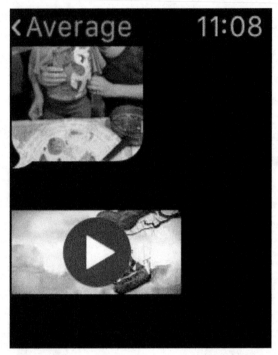

Figure 4: Video in a Text Message

5. Viewing the Text Message Details

You can view the details of a text message, which include the contact's full name, and the options to call or send a text message to the contact. To view the details of a text message:

1. Press the Digital Crown. The Home screen appears, as shown in **Figure 5**.
2. Touch the ⬭ icon. The Messages application opens, as shown in **Figure 6**.
3. Touch the message for which you wish to view details and slide your finger to the left. Touch **Details**. The Text Message Details screen appears, as shown in **Figure 7**.

4. Touch the ![phone icon] icon to call the contact using the speakerphone on the watch. You can also touch the ![message icon] icon to send a new text message to the contact.

Note: You can also view the details of a text message by firmly pressing the screen while viewing a text message.

Figure 5: Home Screen

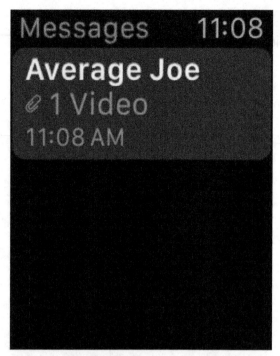

Figure 6: Messages Application

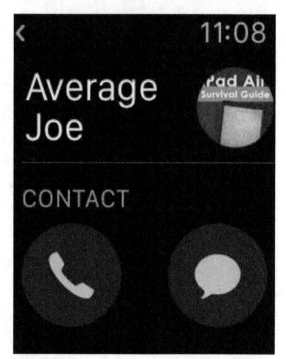

Figure 7: Text Message Details

6. Listening to an Audio Message

iMessage on the iPhone and iPad lets you send a short audio message in a text conversation. When you receive an audio message, it appears in the conversation as shown in **Figure 8**. Touch

the 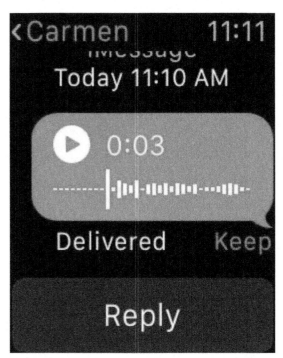 icon to play the audio message.

Figure 8: Audio Message in a Text Conversation

7. Replying to a Text Message

You can reply to a text message from your watch. To reply to a text message:

1. After you receive a text message, touch **Reply** at the bottom of the screen. The Message Reply screen appears, as shown in **Figure 9**.
2. Touch a quick response in the list, or touch one of the following icons at the bottom of the screen:

😃 - Send a custom smiley. Customize the smiley by using the Digital Crown. Swipe left or right to select additional emoticons.

🎤 - Speak your response.

3. Touch **Send**. Your reply is sent.

Figure 9: Message Reply Screen

8. Composing a New Message

You can compose a new text message from your watch. To compose a new message:

1. Press the Digital Crown. The Home screen appears.

2. Touch the ⬜ icon. The Messages application opens.

3. Firmly press the screen, and touch **New Message**. The New Message screen appears, as shown in **Figure 10**.

4. Touch **Add Contact**. A list of contacts whom you have messaged in the past appears.

5. Touch the ⬚ icon at the bottom of the screen. The Phonebook appears, as shown in **Figure 11**.
6. Touch the name of a contact. A list of available numbers appears.
7. Touch a number in the list. The contact is added as a recipient.
8. Touch **Create Message**. The Message Editing screen appears.

9. Touch one of the quick messages, or touch the ☺ icon to dictate your message. You can also touch the 🎤 icon to send a smiley.
10. Touch **Send**. The text message is sent.

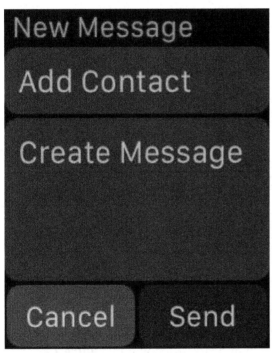

Figure 10: New Message Screen

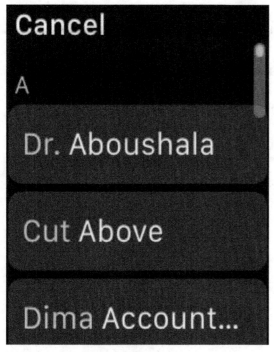

Figure 11: Phonebook

9. Sharing Your Location in a Text Message

You can share your current location on the watch, which is helpful when trying to meet up with a friend. To share your location:

1. Press the Digital Crown. The Home screen appears.

2. Touch the ⬤ icon. The Messages application opens.
3. Touch a conversation in the list. The conversation opens.
4. Firmly press the screen. The Message Options screen appears, as shown in **Figure 12**.
5. Touch **Send Location**. Your location is sent to the selected recipient. The first time that you share your location, touch **Allow** on your iPhone.

Figure 12: Message Options Screen

10. Deleting Text Messages

You can delete text messages from your watch to free up space. To delete a text message:

1. Press the Digital Crown. The Home screen appears.
2. Touch the ⬜ icon. The Messages application opens.
3. Touch the conversation that you want to delete, and slide your finger to the left. 'Details' and 'Trash' appears.
4. Touch **Trash**. A confirmation message appears.
5. Touch **Trash** again. The text conversation is deleted.

Making Calls

Table of Contents

1. Calling a Contact

You can call a contact in your phonebook using the watch. To call a contact:

1. Press the Digital Crown. The Home screen appears, as shown in **Figure 1**.

2. Touch the icon. The Phone application opens, as shown in **Figure 2**.
3. Touch **Contacts**. The Phonebook appears, as shown in **Figure 3**.
4. Touch the name of the contact that you want to call. The Contact screen appears, as shown in **Figure 4**.

5. Touch the icon. The watch calls the selected contact. Use the speakerphone on the watch to talk to the contact. If more than one number is stored in your phonebook for the selected contact, a list of numbers appears. Touch the number that you wish to call.

You can also call a frequently dialed number by pressing the Side button, and touching the name of a contact in your Friends list. Refer to the next section to learn how to add contacts to your friends list.

Figure 1: Home Screen

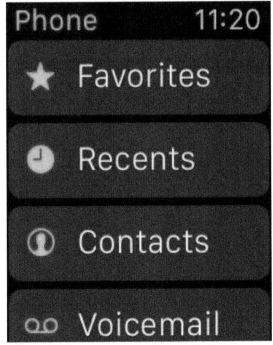

Figure 2: Phone Application

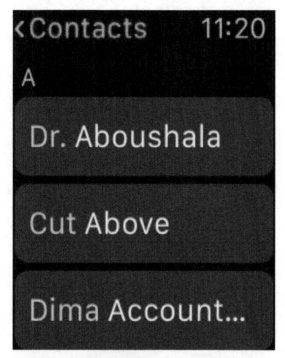

Figure 3: Phonebook on Watch

Figure 4: Contact Screen

2. Adding a Contact to Your Friends List

Add contacts whom you call most often to your friends list, which you can access by pressing the Side button. To add a contact to your friends list:

1. Touch the icon on your iPhone. The Apple Watch Application Home screen appears, as shown in **Figure 5**.
2. Scroll down and touch **Friends**. The Friends screen appears, as shown in **Figure 6**.
3. Touch **Add Friend**. The colored circle to the left of each 'Add Friend' indicates where the friend icon will appear on the watch. The phonebook appears, as shown in **Figure 7**.
4. Touch the name of the contact. The contact is added to your Friends list. You can also

   remove a contact from your Friends list by touching **Edit**, and then touching the icon.

Note: You cannot add a contact to your friends list using the watch.

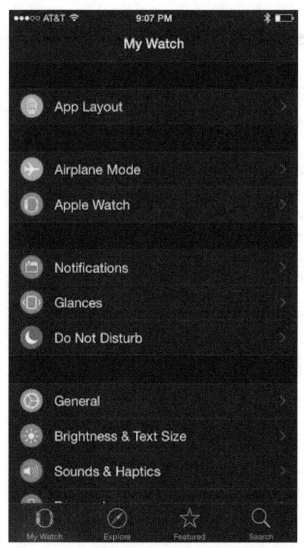

Figure 5: Apple Watch Application Home Screen

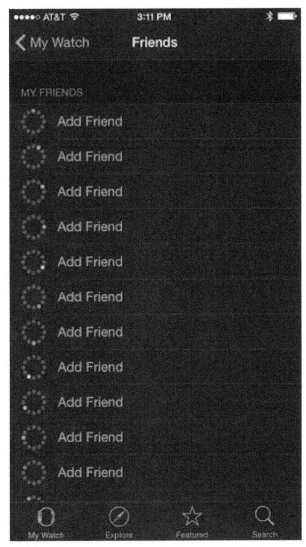

Figure 6: Friends Screen

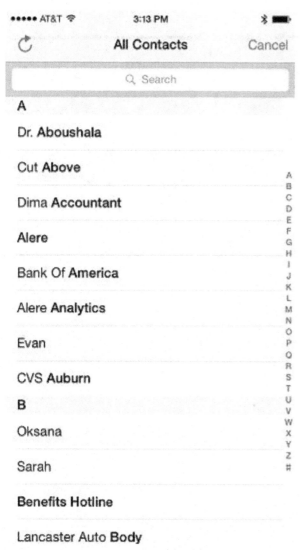

Figure 7: Phonebook on iPhone

3. Returning a Recent Phone Call

You can return recently received, outgoing, missed, or rejected calls. To return a recent phone call:

1. Press the Digital Crown. The Home screen appears.

2. Touch the ![phone icon] icon. The Phone application opens.
3. Touch **Recents**. The Recents screen appears, as shown in **Figure 8**.
4. Touch a number on the screen. The watch dials the number.

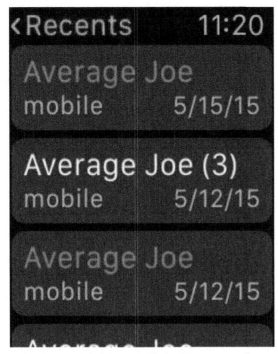

Figure 8: Recents Screen

4. Receiving a Voice Call

When someone calls you, the Incoming Call screen appears, as shown in **Figure 9**. Touch the   icon to answer the call, or touch the   icon to decline it. You can also scroll down and touch **Send a Message** to send a quick text message, or **Answer on iPhone** to answer the call and put it on hold while you take out your iPhone. While the call is on hold, the caller hears a beeping sound.

Figure 9: Incoming Call Screen

5. Listening to Voicemail

You can view your visual voicemail inbox and listen to voicemails on the watch. To listen to a voicemail:

1. Press the Digital Crown. The Home screen appears.

2. Touch the ![icon] icon. The Phone application opens.
3. Touch **Voicemail**. The Voicemail screen appears, as shown in **Figure 10**.
4. Touch the voicemail that you want to hear. The Voicemail Playback screen appears, as shown in **Figure 11**

5. Touch the ![play] button to play the message. You can also touch the ![phone] button to call the contact back, or touch the ![trash] icon to delete the message.

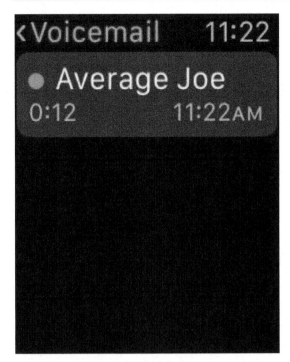

Figure 10: Voicemail Screen

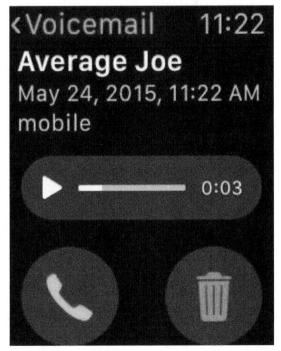

Figure 11: Voicemail Playback Screen

6. Using the Mute Function During a Voice Call

While you are on a call, you can mute your end of the conversation so that the caller cannot hear you. To use the mute function during a voice call, touch the icon. Mute is turned on and the caller cannot hear you. Touch the icon. Mute is turned off, and the caller can hear you again.

7. Viewing Call Information During a Voice Call on the iPhone

While you are on a call on your iPhone, you can view the call information by touching the icon on the Home screen of the watch.

Managing Photos

Table of Contents

1. Selecting a Photo Album on the iPhone

Before you can browse captured or saved photos on the watch, use your iPhone to set the photo album that you want to appear on the watch. To set the photo album:

1. Touch the icon on your iPhone. The Apple Watch Application Home screen appears, as shown in **Figure 1**.
2. Scroll down and touch **Photos**. The Photos screen appears, as shown in **Figure 2**.
3. Touch **Synced Album**. The Synced Album screen appears, as shown in **Figure 3**.
4. Touch the album that you want to appear on the watch. The album is selected, and appears on the watch when you touch the icon.

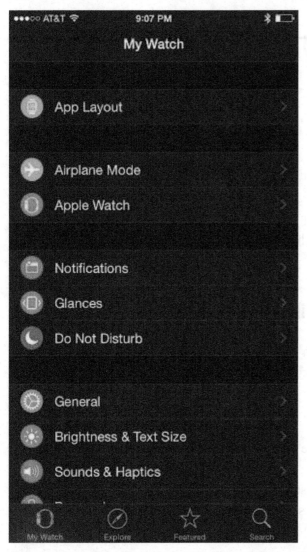

Figure 1: Apple Watch Application Home Screen

Figure 2: Photos Screen

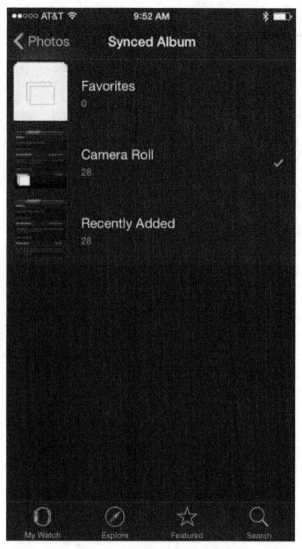

Figure 3: Synced Album Screen

2. Browsing Photos

You can browse captured or saved photos on the watch. To browse photos:

1. Press the Digital Crown. The Home screen appears, as shown in **Figure 4**.

2. Touch the ✿ icon. The Photos application opens.

3. Touch a photo. The photo appears in full screen. You can perform the following actions when viewing a photo:

- Zoom in on or out of the photo by turning the Digital Crown clockwise or counterclockwise, respectively.
- Touch the screen and slide your finger in any direction to view the various parts of the photo when zoomed in.
- Touch the screen two times quickly to return the photo to full-screen view.

Note: The watch cannot display any videos that are stored on your iPhone

Figure 4: Home Screen

3. Set the Photo Storage Limit on the Watch

Since the Apple Watch can only store 6GB of data, you may want to limit the number of photos that are stored on it. If the album that you selected to display on the watch exceeds the limit that you set, only the most recent photos are shown. For example, if you set the limit to 25, only the most recent 25 photos are shown. To set the photo storage limit using your iPhone:

1. Touch the ![icon] icon on your iPhone. The Apple Watch Application Home screen appears.
2. Scroll down and touch **Photos**. The Photos screen appears.

3. Touch **Photos Limit**. The Photos Limit screen appears, as shown in **Figure 5**.
4. Touch the desired photo limit. The number of photos stored on the watch is limited accordingly.

Note: You cannot set the photo storage limit using your watch.

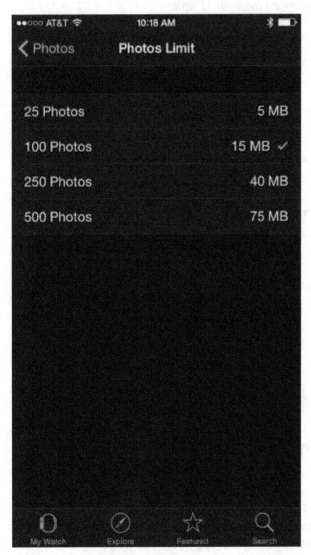

Figure 5: Photos Limit Screen

4. Turn iCloud Photo Sharing Alerts On or Off

When someone connected to your iCloud account (such as family member) shares a photo, the watch can alert you. To turn iCloud Photo Sharing alerts on or off:

1. Touch the [icon] icon on your iPhone. The Apple Watch Application Home screen appears.
2. Scroll down and touch **Photos**. The Photos screen appears.
3. Touch **Custom**. The Alerts option appears.
4. Touch the [switch] switch next to 'Show Alerts'. The [switch] appears, and alerts are turned off.
5. Touch the [switch] switch next to 'Show Alerts'. Alerts are turned on.

Note: You cannot set the iCloud Photo Sharing alerts using your watch.

5. Viewing the Number of Photos on the Watch

You can check how many photos are stored on the watch. To view the number of photos:

1. Press the Digital Crown. The Home screen appears.
2. Touch the [icon] icon. The Settings screen appears, as shown in **Figure 6**.
3. Touch **General**. The General Settings screen appears, as shown in **Figure 7**.
4. Touch **About**. The About screen appears, as shown in **Figure 8**. The number of photos stored on the watch appears on the About screen.

Figure 6: Settings Screen

Figure 7: General Settings Screen

Figure 8: About Screen

Managing Email

Table of Contents

1. Setting the Mailbox to Display on the Watch

By default, the watch uses the first mailbox that you added to your iPhone. If you want to select a different mailbox, use your iPhone. To set the mailbox to display on the watch:

1. Touch the icon on the Home screen of your iPhone. The Apple Watch Application Home screen appears, as shown in **Figure 1**.
2. Scroll down and touch **Mail**. The Mail screen appears, as shown in **Figure 2**.
3. Touch **Include Mail**. The Include Mail screen appears, as shown in **Figure 3**.
4. Touch the mailbox that you want to show on the watch. The mailbox is selected, and the email that it contains appears in the Mail application on the watch.

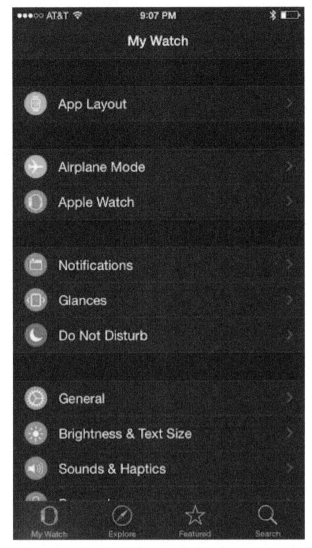

Figure 1: Apple Watch Application Home Screen

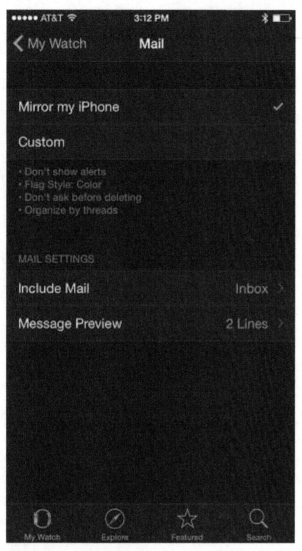

Figure 2: Mail Screen

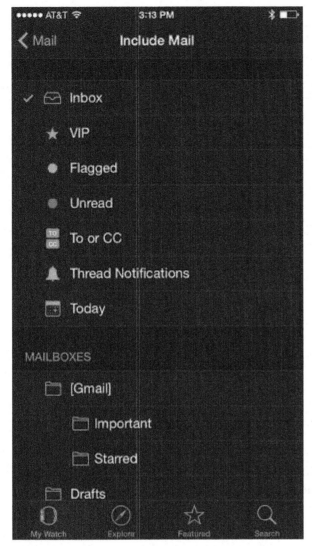

Figure 3: Include Mail Screen

2. Reading Email

You can read your email on the watch. To read email:

1. Press the Digital Crown. The Home screen appears.
2. Touch the ✉ icon. The Inbox appears, as shown in **Figure 4**.
3. Touch an email in the inbox. The email opens.
4. Use the Digital Crown to scroll through the email quickly. You can also touch the top of the screen to immediately scroll to the top of the email.

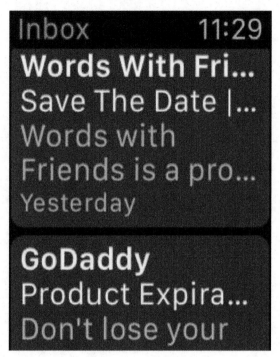

Figure 4: Inbox

3. Viewing Email Details

If the name of the sender or the list of recipients is too long to fit on the screen, you can touch the name of the sender at the top of the email to view more details.

4. Mark an Email as Unread

If you opened an email, but do not have time to read it, you can mark it as 'Unread'. To mark an email as unread:

1. Firmly press the screen when viewing an email. The Email options appear, as shown in **Figure 5**.
2. Touch **Unread**. The email appears as a new message in your Inbox, which is signified by a blue dot.
3. Firmly press the email again, and touch **Read**. The email is marked as 'Read'.

Figure 5: Email Options

5. Flag an Email

If you read an email, and you want to follow up later, you can flag it. To flag an email, firmly press the screen while viewing it, and touch **Flag**. A red dot appears next to the subject, which acts as the flag. Firmly press the screen again, and touch **Unflag**. The flag is removed.

6. Archive an Email

You may want to archive emails to free up space on the watch. Archiving an email removes it from your Inbox, placing it in the All Mail folder that does not take up space on your iPhone or watch. To archive an email, touch the email in the Inbox, and slide your finger to the left. The Message options appear. Touch **Archive**. The email is archived, and can be found in the 'All Mail' folder.

7. Adjust the Email Alert Settings

If you prefer not to be notified when a new email arrives, you can turn email alerts off. To turn email alerts on or off:

1. Touch the ![icon] icon on the Home screen of your iPhone. The Apple Watch Application Home screen appears.
2. Scroll down and touch **Mail**. The Mail screen appears.
3. Touch **Custom**. The Alerts options appear.
4. Touch the ![switch] switch next to 'Show Alerts'. Alerts are turned off.
5. Touch the ![switch] switch next to 'Show Alerts'. Alerts are turned on.

Listening to Music

Table of Contents

1. Controlling Music on Your iPhone

You can start music playback on your iPhone using your watch. To play music on your iPhone:

1. Press the Digital Crown. The Home screen appears, as shown in **Figure 1**.

2. Touch the [icon] icon. The Music application opens, as shown in **Figure 2**.

3. Touch **Artists**, **Albums**, **Songs**, or **Playlists** to select music. A list of songs appears.

4. Touch a song. The music begins to play on the iPhone. If you do not hear music on the iPhone, press the screen firmly, and touch **Source**. Then, touch **iPhone**.

5. Touch one of the following buttons to control the music:

[⏸] - Pause the song.

[⏮] - Skip to the beginning of the song, or to the previous song in the album or playlist, if less than five seconds of the current song have played.

[⏭] - Skip to the next song in the album or playlist.

Use the Digital Crown on your watch to control the volume of the speaker on your iPhone.

Figure 1: Home Screen

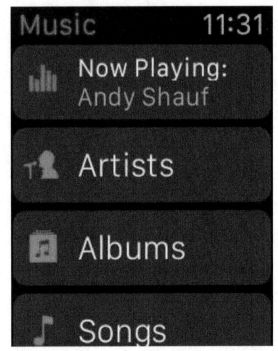

Figure 2: Music Application

2. Transferring Music to Your Watch

To listen to music that is stored on your watch, transfer one or more playlists to the watch. To transfer music to your watch:

1. Touch the icon on your iPhone. The Apple Watch Application Home screen appears, as shown in **Figure 3**.
2. Scroll down and touch **Music**. The Music screen appears, as shown in **Figure 4**.
3. Touch **Synced Playlist**. The Synced Playlist screen appears, as shown in **Figure 5**.
4. Touch the playlist that you want to sync. The playlist is ready to sync.
5. Place your watch on its charging dock. The playlist is transferred to your watch.

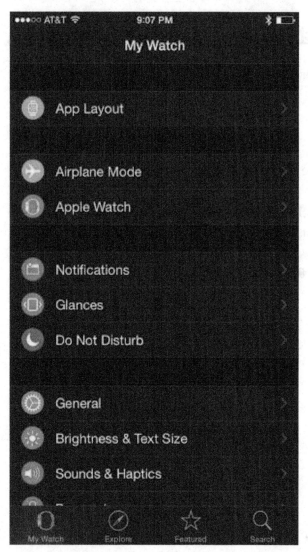

Figure 3: Apple Watch Application Home Screen

Figure 4: Music Screen

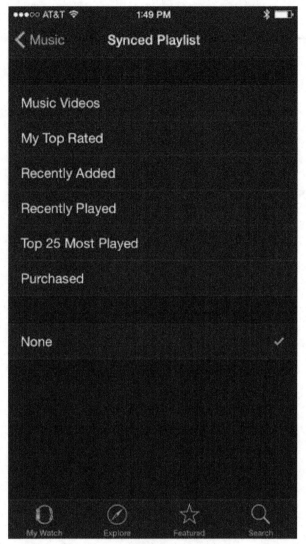

Figure 5: Synced Playlist Screen

3. Listening to Music on Your Watch

To listen to music on your watch, first connect the watch to a Bluetooth headset or speaker. To connect the watch to a headset or speaker:

1. Press the Digital Crown. The Home screen appears.

2. Touch the ⚙ icon. The Settings screen appears, as shown in **Figure 6**.

3. Touch **Bluetooth**. The Bluetooth screen appears, as shown in **Figure 7**.

4. Ensure that your headset or speaker is discoverable. Refer to the documentation for your device to learn how to make it visible by other devices.
5. Touch the name of a device under 'Devices'. The watch connects to the device.

To listen to music stored on your watch:

1. Press the Digital Crown. The Home screen appears.
2. Touch the 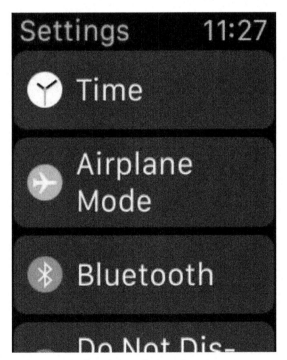 icon. The Music application opens.
3. Press the screen firmly. The Music options appear, as shown in **Figure 8**.
4. Touch **Source**. 'iPhone' and 'Apple Watch' appear.
5. Touch **Apple Watch**. The music stored on your watch appears. Refer to *"Controlling Music on Your iPhone"* on page 57 to learn how to listen to music.

Figure 6: Settings Screen

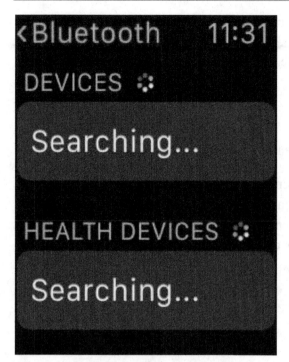

Figure 7: Bluetooth Screen

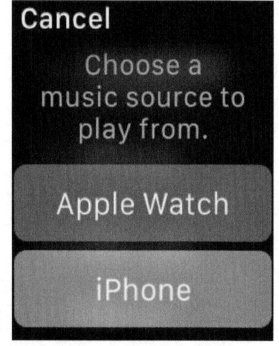

Figure 8: Music Options

4. Limiting the Number of Stored Songs on the Watch

To prevent accidentally loading too much music on your watch, you can limit the number of songs that can be transferred to it. To limit the number of stored songs:

1. Touch the icon on your iPhone. The Apple Watch Application Home screen appears.
2. Scroll down and touch **Music**. The Music screen appears.
3. Touch **Playlist Limit**. The Playlist Limit screen appears, as shown in **Figure 9**.
4. Touch **Storage** or **Songs** to select the unit of measure for the limit.
5. Touch the desired limit. The limit is set.

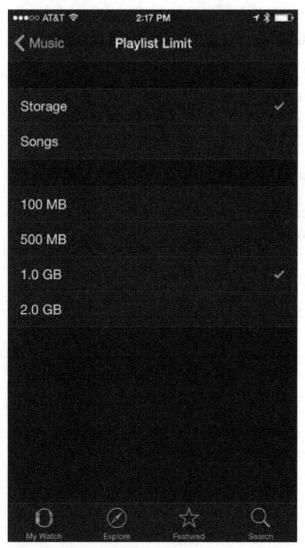

Figure 9: Playlist Limit Screen

Staying Fit

Table of Contents

1. Setting Up the Fitness Application

Before you can track your daily activity and record workouts, set up the fitness application. To set up the application for the first time:

1. Press the Digital Crown. The Home screen appears, as shown in **Figure 1**.

2. Touch the icon. The Fitness application opens.

3. Touch **OK**, and then swipe to the right until 'Get Started' appears.

4. Touch **Get Started**. The Personal Information screen appears, as shown in **Figure 2**. If you have already entered your personal information, the Activity screen appears, as shown in **Figure 3**. In this case, skip to step 6.

5. Enter your personal information, and touch **Continue**. The Activity screen appears.

6. Touch **Lightly**, **Moderately**, or **Highly**. The Calorie screen appears, as shown in **Figure 4**.

7. Touch the + and - buttons to adjust your daily calorie goal, and touch **Start Moving**. Your fitness application is ready to use.

Figure 1: Home Screen

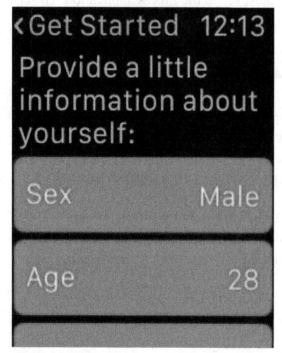

Figure 2: Personal Information Screen

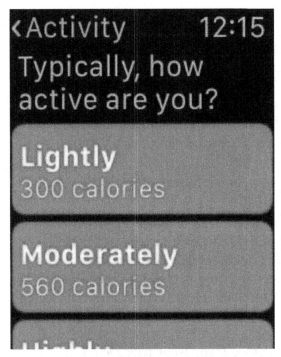

Figure 3: Activity Screen

Figure 4: Calorie Screen

2. Tracking Daily Activity

The Fitness application lets you track the number of steps that you have taken, the number of hours that you have stood up, and the number of calories that you have burned. To track your daily activity:

1. Touch the watch face and slide your finger up. The Glance screen appears, and varies based on the last screen that you opened (such as the calendar, heart rate, or weather screen).
2. Touch the screen and slide your finger to the left or right until the Daily Activity screen appears, as shown in **Figure 5**.
3. Touch the Daily Activity screen. The Move screen appears, as shown in **Figure 6**.
4. Touch the screen and slide your finger to the left or right to view the number of calories that you have burned (Calorie screen), the number of minutes that you have exercised (Exercise screen), and the number of hours that you have stood at least once during the hour (Stand screen). Slide your finger up to view more details, such as the number of steps that you have taken.

Note: The pedometer on the Apple Watch is extremely sensitive. If you wear your watch while typing or doing another activity that causes your wrist to move excessively, the number of steps that you have taken each day may not register correctly.

Figure 5: Daily Activity Screen

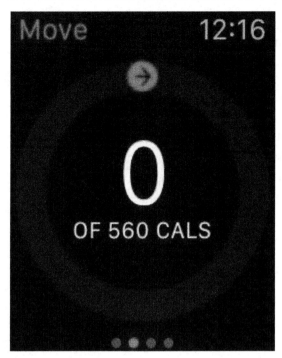

Figure 6: Move Screen

3. Adjust Your Fitness Goal

You can change your fitness goals at any time. To adjust your fitness goals, press the screen firmly on the Calorie screen, Exercise screen, or Stand screen. Touch **Change Move Goal**. The only adjustable fitness goal is the number of calories that you want to burn during each day.

4. Record a Workout

The watch can track your workouts and record your results. To record a workout:

1. Press the Digital Crown. The Home screen appears.

2. Touch the 🏃 icon. The Fitness application opens and the list of workout types appears, as shown in **Figure 7**.
3. Touch the type of workout that you are about to start. The Workout Calorie screen appears.

4. Adjust the number of calories, or touch the screen and slide your finger to the right to set a specific time or distance for the workout. You can also set the workout to be open, which lets you stop it at any time. You cannot set a distance goal if you are doing an elliptical, rower, or stair stepper workout.

5. Touch **Start**. The workout begins.

6. During the workout, slide your finger to the left or right on the screen to view your progress. The leftmost screen lets you pause or stop the workout. If you set a specific goal, the workout ends automatically once you have met that goal.

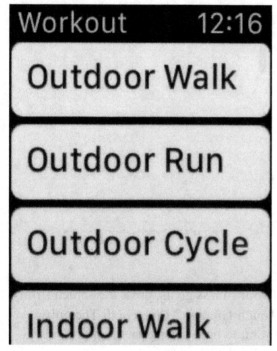

Figure 7: List of Workout Types

5. Checking Your Heart Rate

To check your heart rate at any time, touch the watch face (Clock) and slide your finger up. Ensure that the watch is secured on your wrist. Then, slide your finger to the left or right until 'Heart Rate' appears. Your heart rate appears after a few moments, as shown in **Figure 8**.

Figure 8: Heart Rate

6. Set Your Height and Weight

To accurately determine the number of calories that you have burned, ensure that you keep your height and weight records up-to-date. To set your height and weight:

1. Touch the  icon on the Home screen of your iPhone. The Apple Watch Application Home screen appears, as shown in **Figure 9**.
2. Scroll down and touch **Health**. The Health screen appears, as shown in **Figure 10**.
3. Touch **Edit** at the top of the screen. You can now edit the height and weight.
4. Touch the height or weight, and use the adjustment slider at the bottom of the screen.
5. Touch **Done** at the top of the screen. The height and weight are adjusted accordingly.

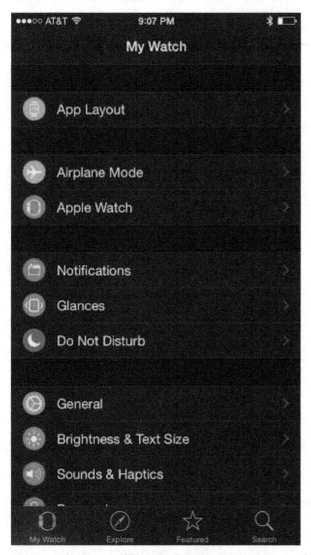

Figure 9: Apple Watch Application Home Screen

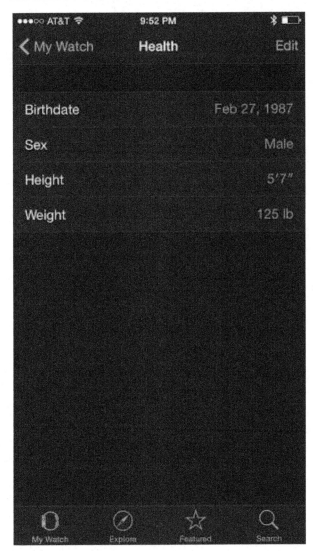

Figure 10: Health Screen

7. Adjusting Activity Notifications

You can turn on activity notifications to remind you to stand, or to show you progress updates or achievements. To adjust activity notifications:

1. Touch the icon on the Home screen of your iPhone. The Apple Watch Application Home screen appears.
2. Touch **Notifications**. The Notifications screen appears, as shown in **Figure 11**.
3. Touch **Activity**. The Activity Settings screen appears, as shown in **Figure 12**.

4. Touch the switch or switch next to one of the options to turn it on or off.

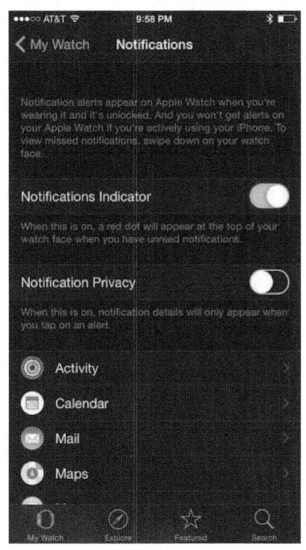

Figure 11: Notifications Screen

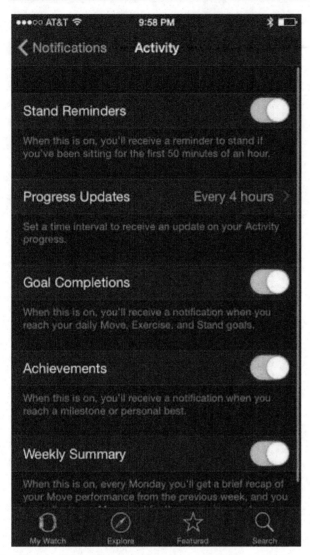

Figure 12: Activity Settings Screen

Adjusting the Settings

Table of Contents

1. Adjusting Watch Orientation Settings

The orientation of the display on the watch varies depending on the wrist on which you are wearing it, and the location of the crown when you look at the watch. To adjust watch orientation settings:

1. Press the Digital Crown. The Home screen appears, as shown in **Figure 1**.

2. Touch the 🔘 icon. The Settings screen appears, as shown in **Figure 2**.

3. Scroll down and touch **General**. The General Settings screen appears, as shown in **Figure 3**.

4. Touch **Orientation**. The Orientation screen appears, as shown in **Figure 4**.

5. Touch **Left** or **Right** under 'Wrist' or 'Crown' to adjust the corresponding setting. The new orientation settings are saved.

Figure 1: Home Screen

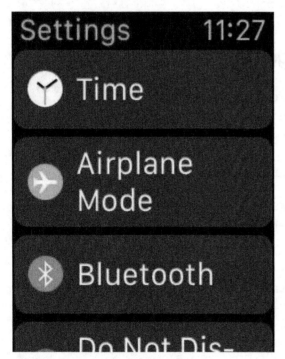

Figure 2: Settings Screen

Figure 3: General Settings Screen

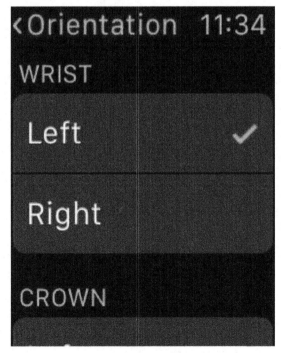

Figure 4: Orientation Screen

2. Adjusting Wrist Raise Settings

The watch can automatically turn on when you raise your wrist to look at it. You can also set the watch to either show the clock face or the application that was used last. By default, Wrist Raise is turned on. To adjust wrist raise settings:

1. Press the Digital Crown. The Home screen appears.
2. Touch the ⊚ icon. The Settings screen appears.
3. Scroll down and touch **General**. The General Settings screen appears.
4. Touch **Activate on Wrist Raise**. The Wrist Raise Settings screen appears, as shown in **Figure 5**.
5. Touch **Wrist Raise**. The Wrist Raise feature is turned off.
6. Touch **Wrist Raise** again. The Wrist Raise feature is turned on.
7. Scroll down and touch **Last Used App** to have the watch display the application that you were using when the watch went to sleep. Otherwise, touch **Clock Face** to view the time when you raise your wrist.

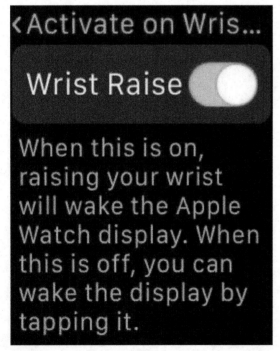

Figure 5: Wrist Raise Settings Screen

3. Adjusting Accessibility Settings

There are several accessibility features that can be turned on for those with visual impairments. To adjust accessibility settings:

1. Press the Digital Crown. The Home screen appears.
2. Touch the 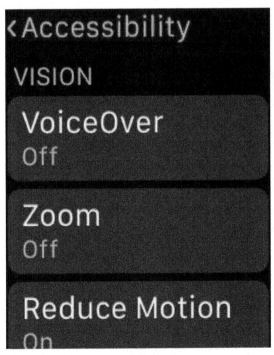 icon. The Settings screen appears.
3. Scroll down and touch **General**. The General Settings screen appears.
4. Touch **Accessibility.** The Accessibility Settings screen appears, as shown in **Figure 6**.
5. Touch one of the following options to turn it on or off:

   - **VoiceOver** - Speaks an item on the screen when you touch it. To select an item, touch it or swipe to the left or right. Touch an item twice quickly to select it.
   - **Zoom** - Zooms in on a location on the screen when you touch it twice quickly with two fingers.
   - **Reduce Motion** - Speeds up transitions between screens to reduce the animation effect.
   - **On/Off Labels** - Applies the I and O labels to the On and Off switches.

Figure 6: Accessibility Settings

4. Turning Quick Siri Activation On or Off

There are two ways to turn on Siri: press and hold the Digital Crown or raise your wrist and say "Hey Siri." If you are having trouble turning on Siri using your voice, make sure that voice activation for Siri is turned on. To turn the feature on or off:

1. Press the Digital Crown. The Home screen appears.
2. Touch the ⚙ icon. The Settings screen appears.
3. Scroll down and touch **General**. The General Settings screen appears.
4. Touch **Siri**. The Siri settings screen appears, as shown in **Figure 7**.
5. Touch **Hey Siri**. The ⬤ switch appears, and voice activation for Siri is turned on.
6. Touch **Hey Siri**. The ⬤ switch appears, and voice activation for Siri is turned off.

Figure 7: Siri Settings Screen

5. Resetting the Watch to Factory Defaults

If you experience problems with your watch, or if you want to transfer it to another owner, it is a good idea to reset the watch. To reset the watch to factory defaults:

Warning: If you reset the watch to factory defaults, all of your data and settings are permanently erased.

1. Press the Digital Crown. The Home screen appears.
2. Touch the 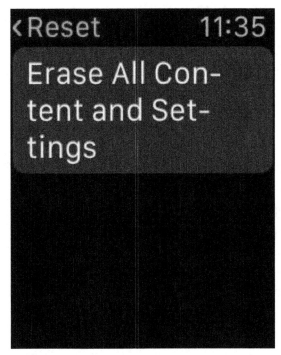 icon. The Settings screen appears.
3. Scroll down and touch **General**. The General Settings screen appears.
4. Touch **Reset**. The Reset screen appears, as shown in **Figure 8**.
5. Touch **Erase All Content and Settings**. A confirmation screen appears.
6. Touch **Continue**. The watch is reset. After the reset is complete, pair the watch with an iPhone before using it.

Figure 8: Reset Screen

6. Turning Airplane Mode On or Off

Putting the watch in Airplane mode turns off Bluetooth, which allows the watch to connect to an iPhone. However, you can still use functions that do not require the iPhone normally. Refer to *"What the Apple Watch Can and Cannot Do"* on page 5 to learn about the functions that you can use without an iPhone. Use Airplane mode to save battery life or while flying. To turn Airplane mode on or off:

1. Press the Digital Crown. The Home screen appears.

2. Touch the   icon. The Settings screen appears.
3. Touch **Airplane Mode**. The Airplane Mode screen appears.

4. Touch **Airplane Mode**. The   switch appears, and Airplane Mode is turned on.

5. Touch **Airplane Mode**. The   switch appears, and Airplane Mode is turned off.

7. Unpairing the Watch

If you want to pair the watch to another iPhone, first unpair the watch from the current one. To unpair the watch:

1. Touch the   icon on your iPhone. The Apple Watch Application Home screen appears, as shown in **Figure 9**.
2. Touch **Apple Watch**. The Apple Watch screen appears, as shown in **Figure 10**.
3. Touch **Unpair Apple Watch**. A confirmation appears at the bottom of the screen.
4. Touch **Unpair NAME Apple Watch**, where NAME is the name that you used when setting up your iTunes account. The watch is unpaired from your iPhone. Refer to *"Setting Up"* on page 7 to learn how to pair the watch to another iPhone.

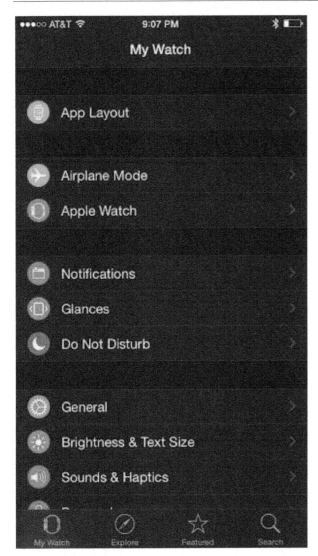

Figure 9: Apple Watch Application Home Screen

Figure 10: Apple Watch Screen

8. Customizing the Glances Screen

The Glances screen appears when you touch the clock face and slide your finger up. This screen lets you quickly preview fitness goals, weather, calendar events, and more. To customize the screens that appear on the Glances screen:

1. Touch the ![icon] icon on your iPhone. The Apple Watch Application Home screen appears.

2. Touch **Glances**. The Glances screen appears, as shown in **Figure 11**.

3. Touch the ![icon] icon next to any item that you want to remove. 'Remove' appears.

4. Touch **Remove**. The item is removed from the Glances screen.

5. To add an item to the Glances screen, touch the ![icon] icon. The new item is added. If you do not see an ![icon] icon, all of the items have already been added to the Glances screen.

Note: Not all applications are compatible with Glances.

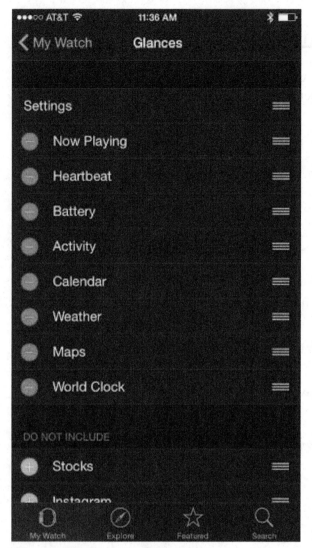

Figure 11: Glances Screen

9. Adjusting the Brightness and Text Size

If you are having trouble seeing the text or images on the screen, try increasing the brightness or text size. To adjust the brightness and text size:

1. Press the Digital Crown. The Home screen appears.
2. Touch the ⊚ icon. The Settings screen appears.
3. Touch **Brightness & Text Size**. The Brightness & Text Size settings screen appears, as shown in **Figure 12**.

4. Touch the ![brightness bar] bar, and use the Digital Crown to adjust the brightness. The new brightness setting is saved.

5. Touch **Text Size**. The Text Size screen appears.

6. Touch the ![text size bar] bar, and use the Digital Crown to adjust the font size. The new font setting is saved.

Figure 12: Brightness & Text Size Settings Screen

10. Adjusting the Sound and Vibration

You can adjust the volume and vibration settings on the watch. To adjust sound and vibration:

1. Press the Digital Crown. The Home screen appears.

2. Touch the ⚙ icon. The Settings screen appears.

3. Touch **Sounds & Haptics**. The Sounds & Haptics screen appears, as shown in **Figure 13**.

4. You can adjust the following settings on this screen:

- Touch the [image: volume bar] bar, and use the Digital Crown to adjust the volume.
- Touch **Mute** to turn off all sounds except alarms.
- Touch **Prominent Haptic** to turn on a more intense vibration alert when a call or text is received.

Figure 13: Sounds & Haptics Screen

11. Setting Up a Security Passcode

If you have sensitive data on your watch, you may want to protect it with a passcode. After you set up a passcode, you have to enter it every time that you want to unlock your watch. To set up a security passcode:

1. Touch the [icon] icon on your iPhone. The Apple Watch Application Home screen appears.
2. Touch **Passcode**. The Passcode screen appears, as shown in **Figure 14**.

3. Touch **Turn Passcode On**. The Passcode Creation screen appears on your watch, as shown in **Figure 15**.

4. Enter the passcode twice. The passcode is set. If you want to turn off the passcode, touch **Turn Passcode Off** on the Passcode screen on the iPhone.

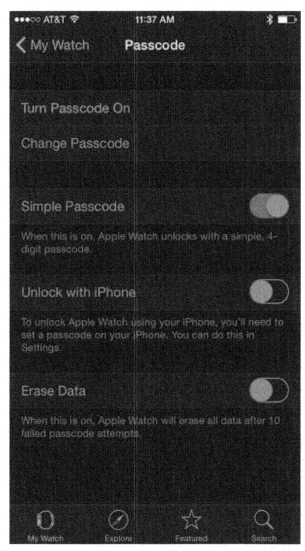

Figure 14: Passcode Screen

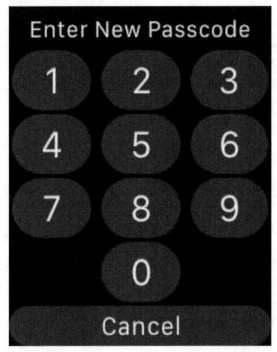

Figure 15: Passcode Creation Screen

12. Setting the Time Ahead on the Clock Face

If you want to set the clock face to display a time other than the current time, you can set the time up to 59 minutes ahead. To set the time ahead on the clock face:

1. Press the Digital Crown. The Home screen appears.
2. Touch the ⚙ icon. The Settings screen appears.
3. Touch **Time**. The Time screen appears, as shown in **Figure 16**.
4. Touch **+0 Min**. The Time Adjustment screen appears, as shown in **Figure 17**.
5. Turn the Digital Crown clockwise or counterclockwise to set the time forward or back, respectively. The time will be displayed accordingly on the watch face.

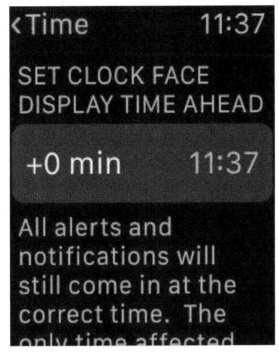

Figure 16: Time Screen

Figure 17: Time Adjustment Screen

Tips and Tricks

Table of Contents

1. Maximizing Battery Life

There are many things that you can do to increase the battery life of the watch:

- Choose a watch face that is mostly black, such as the analog face. Showing more black on the screen consumes less battery life.

- Turn off the notifications that you do not need. To turn off notifications, touch the icon on your iPhone, and then touch **Notifications**.
- Turn down the sound or mute the watch completely. Refer to *"Adjusting the Sound and Vibration"* on page 91 to learn how.
- Turn off Prominent Haptic feedback to turn off strong vibrations. Refer to *"Adjusting the Sound and Vibration"* on page 91 to learn how.
- Turn off Wrist Raise, as it can often accidentally turns on the watch screen.
- Turn on the Power Reserve feature, which puts the watch in a low-power state that only shows time. Touch **Power Reserve** on the Battery Glance screen. Swipe up from the watch face and move your finger to the left or right to find the Battery Glance screen.
- Turn down the brightness. Refer to *"Adjusting the Brightness and Text Size"* on page 90 to learn how.

- Do not make calls using the watch. Using the speakerphone on the watch can quickly kill the battery.
- Turn off the "Hey Siri" feature, which causes the watch to always listen for the phrase when it is unlocked. Refer to *"Turning Quick Siri Activation On or Off"* on page 84 to learn how.
- Do not use the alarm feature.
- If you do not need notifications while you sleep, turn off your watch while it is charging.
- Add the battery indicator to your watch face to keep a closer eye on your battery life. To view the battery indicator, customize your watch face. Refer to *"Customizing the Clock"* on page 11 to learn how.

2. Finding Your iPhone Using Your Watch

If you ever lose your phone in your home, you can use your watch to find it. To find your iPhone using your watch, slide your finger up on the watch face. The Glances screen appears. Move your finger to the left or right until you see 'Connected', and touch the icon. The iPhone emits a loud beep, even if it is in Vibration mode.

3. Using the Siri Voice Assistant

You can use Siri to perform various tasks, such as setting a timer or playing music. There are two ways to activate Siri: press and hold the Digital Crown or say "Hey Siri". If saying "Hey Siri" does not work, ensure that the function is turned on. Refer to *"Turning Quick Siri Activation On or Off"* on page 84 to learn how.

4. Setting an Alarm

If you like to wear your watch while you sleep, the Apple watch can wake you up with a tap (vibration) on your wrist. To set an alarm:

1. Press the Digital Crown. The Home screen appears.
2. Touch the icon. The Alarm application opens.
3. Press the screen firmly, and touch **New**. The New Alarm screen appears.
4. Touch **Change time**. The Alarm Settings screen appears.

5. Use the Digital Crown to adjust the time. Touch **Set** when you are finished. The alarm is set. Touch the alarm on the Alarms screen, and touch **Delete** at the bottom of the screen that appears to remove it.

Note: The watch does not make a sound when the alarm goes off.

5. Using the Watch as a Viewfinder for Your iPhone Camera

To take a group picture with your iPhone, you can use the viewfinder feature. This feature lets you use your watch to look through the lens of your iPhone. To use viewfinder:

1. Make sure that your iPhone is turned on.
2. Press the Digital Crown. The Home screen appears.
3. Touch the icon. The viewfinder turns on, and the camera turns on automatically on your iPhone.
4. Touch the button to take the picture, or touch **3S** to set a three-second timer. The picture is captured. You can also touch the watch screen anywhere to make the iPhone automatically focus on a specific point.

6. Taking a Screenshot

If you want to capture the image that is on the screen, press and quickly release the Digital Crown and Side Button. The screen briefly flashes a white color, and a screenshot is captured. All screenshots that you capture on the watch are stored in your photo album on the iPhone.

7. Restarting the Watch

If the watch is not responding, or is behaving strangely, try restarting it. To restart the watch, press and hold the Digital Crown and Side Button simultaneously. Keep holding the buttons until the Apple logo appears. Release the buttons, and the watch restarts.

8. Muting Watch Alerts with Your Palm

When an alert comes in on your watch, you can mute it by covering the screen with your palm. To

turn on this feature, touch the icon on your iPhone, and then touch **Sounds & Haptics**.

Touch the switch next to 'Cover to Mute'. The switch appears, and the feature is turned on.

9. Customizing Quick Text Message Responses

When you receive a text message, you can respond with one of several preset messages, which can be customized. To customize quick text message responses:

1. Touch the icon on your iPhone, and then touch **Messages**. The Messages screen appears.
2. Touch **Default Replies**. The Default Replies screen appears.
3. Touch a field under 'Default Replies' and enter your desired message.
4. Touch **Messages** at the top of the screen. Your default replies are saved.

10. Continuing to Work on Your iPhone

The watch lets you start working in an application, and then continue where you left off using your iPhone. This feature is known as Handoff. For example, if you start viewing an email, you may want to switch to the iPhone to reply to it. By default, Handoff is turned on. If you turned it off,

turn it on by touching the icon on your iPhone, and then touching **General**. On the

General screen, touch the switch next to 'Enable Handoff'. To use Handoff, start using the application on your watch. On the lockscreen of your iPhone, touch the application icon in the lower left-hand corner of the screen, and slide your finger up. The iPhone picks up where you left off on the watch.

Note: When you lock the iPhone for the first time after using Handoff, the application icon no longer appears in the lower left-hand corner.

11. Clearing All Notifications at Once

If you have many notifications in your list when you slide your finger down from the top of the screen, you may want to clear them all. To clear all notifications at once, press the screen firmly while viewing your notifications. Touch **Clear All**. All notifications are removed.

Troubleshooting

Table of Contents

1. Watch is not responding

If the watch stops responding, try restarting it. To restart the watch, press and hold the Digital Crown and Side Button at the same time until the Apple logo appears.

2. Watch cannot communicate with the iPhone

If the watch indicates that it cannot find the iPhone, but you have paired the watch to the iPhone, there may be a Bluetooth issue. To resolve this problem, turn Bluetooth off and back on on the iPhone. The fastest way to do this is to slide your finger up from the bottom of the screen, and

touch the icon.

3. iPhone battery dies quickly when connected to the watch

The battery on your iPhone may die more quickly when the phone is paired with the watch. Use the following tips if you notice a decrease in battery life on your iPhone:

- Restart both the iPhone and the watch. Refer to *"Turning the Apple Watch On or Off"* on page 10 to learn how to restart the watch. To restart the iPhone, press and hold the Power button until 'Slide to power off' appears. Touch the ⏻ icon and slide it to the right. Then, turn on your iPhone.
- Close the Apple Watch application on your iPhone when you are not using it. To close an application, press the Home button twice quickly and find the Apple Watch application on the multitasking screen. Slide your finger up until the application disappears.

4. Stainless steel watch is easily scratched

Although Apple claims that the watch is difficult to scratch, stainless steel is known for being very soft and easy to scratch. Luckily, it is easy to remove any scratches by using a metal polish, such as **Mag & Aluminum Polish**, and a towel. Clean the watch, and rub the polish on the scratched surface. The polish does not damage the watch in any way.

5. Watch is malfunctioning with a dark tattoo

If you have a dark tattoo on your wrist, the watch may not be able to detect that you have a pulse. One fix that is suggested for this issue is to turn off the Wrist Detection feature, which turns on the watch screen when you raise your wrist. To turn off the Wrist Detection feature:

1. Touch the ▢ icon on your iPhone. The Apple Watch Application Home screen appears.
2. Touch **General**. The General Settings screen appears.
3. Touch the ⬤ switch next to 'Wrist Detection'. The feature is turned off.

6. Watch is performing slowly

If the watch performance is slowing down, try uninstalling some of the applications. Filling up the memory too much can cause performance issues on some watches. Refer to *"Deleting an Installed Application"* on page 17 to learn more.

7. Pedometer does not report step count correctly

The pedometer on the watch does not always function correctly, and may count many more steps than you actually take. There is no known fix for this issue. Try to use another device as your pedometer.

8. Watch does not charge

If the watch does not charge when you place it on the charging dock, try restarting it. Refer to *"Turning the Apple Watch On or Off"* on page 10 to learn how. If the watch still does not charge, try resetting it to factory defaults. Refer to *"Resetting the Watch to Factory Defaults"* on page 85 to learn how.

9. What to do if your problem is not listed here

If you could not resolve your problem, contact Apple Support using one of the following methods:
Phone: 800-275-2273
Online: www.apple.com/support/watch/

Index

Other Books from the Author of the Help Me Series, Charles Hughes

Help Me! Guide to the iPad Air

Help Me! Guide to the iPad Air 2

Help Me! Guide to the iOS 8

Help Me! Guide to the iPhone 5S

Help Me! Guide to the iPhone 6

Help Me! Guide to the iPhone 4

Help Me! Guide to the Nexus 7

Help Me! Guide to the Galaxy S4

Help Me! Guide to the Kindle Fire HD

Help Me! Guide to the HTC One

Help Me! Guide to the iPod Touch

Help Me! Guide to the iPad Mini

Help Me! Guide to the Kindle Touch

Help Me! Guide to the Samsung Galaxy Note

Help Me! Guide to the Kindle Fire HD 6

Help Me! Guide to the Kindle Fire TV

Help Me! Guide to the Nexus 5

Help Me! Guide to the Samsung Galaxy Note 3

Help Me! Guide to the Apple Watch

Author: Charles Hughes

This book is also available in electronic format from Amazon.com

CPSIA information can be obtained at www.ICGtesting.com
Printed in the USA
LVOW02s0151100615

441861LV00002B/23/P